American Paint Horses

by Grace Hansen

Abdo
HORSES
Kids

abdopublishing.com

Published by Abdo Kids, a division of ABDO, P.O. Box 398166, Minneapolis, Minnesota 55439.

Copyright © 2017 by Abdo Consulting Group, Inc. International copyrights reserved in all countries. No part of this book may be reproduced in any form without written permission from the publisher.

Printed in the United States of America, North Mankato, Minnesota.

102016

012017

Photo Credits: Alamy, Animals Animals, iStock, Shutterstock

Production Contributors: Teddy Borth, Jennie Forsberg, Grace Hansen

Design Contributors: Dorothy Toth, Laura Mitchell

Publisher's Cataloging in Publication Data

Names: Hansen, Grace, author.

Title: American paint horses / by Grace Hansen.

Description: Minneapolis, Minnesota : Abdo Kids, 2017 | Series: Horses | Includes bibliographical references and index.

Identifiers: LCCN 2016944091 | ISBN 9781680809251 (lib. bdg.) | ISBN 9781680796353 (ebook) | ISBN 9781680797022 (Read-to-me ebook)

Subjects: LCSH: American paint horses--Juvenile literature.

Classification: DDC 636.1/3--dc23

LC record available at http://lccn.loc.gov/2016944091

Table of Contents

American Paint Horses

Spotting an American Paint Horse is easy. Its grace and beautiful coat make it stand out.

American Paints are **sturdy**, powerful horses. Their strong **hindquarters** help them move quickly.

Paint Horses come in many colors. Black, brown, and **roan** are just a few. All Paint Horses have white markings, too.

Paint Horses come in two main **patterns**. One is the tobiano pattern. A tobiano horse has spots on its body. Each leg is white below the knee. The tail is two colors.

Overo is the second **pattern**. An overo horse has at least one dark leg. It has markings on its head and body. The tail is usually one color.

13

Native Americans **tamed** Paint
Horses long ago. They loved
the horse for both its beauty
and smarts.

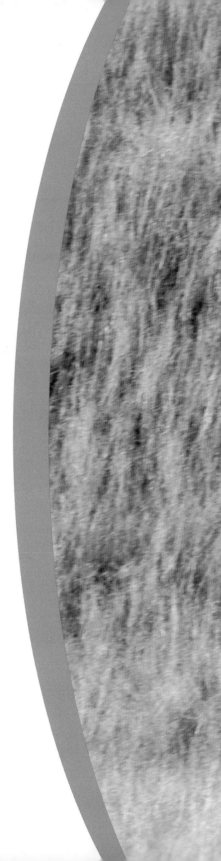

American Paints have always
been naturals at herding cattle.
Cowboys in the Old West used
them for ranch work.

A Horse of Many Talents

Today's American Paint Horse is still very smart. It is also easy to train. These things, along with its good nature, make it able to do just about anything.

19

American Paints work on ranches and farms. They also excel at riding, racing, rodeo, and more!

21

More Facts

- Some Paint Horses have features from both the overo and tobiano **patterns**. So they are said to have the tovero pattern.

- No two Paint Horses have the exact same markings.

- The American Paint shares common **ancestors** with the quarter horse and the thoroughbred.

Glossary

ancestor – someone or something that lived years ago that is related to a certain person or animal living today.

hindquarters – the rear part of an animal.

pattern – a repeated marking.

roan – a base color sprinkled with white or gray hairs.

sturdy – strongly made.

tame – to take from being a wild animal to a domesticated animal.

23

Index

abdokids.com

Use this code to log on to abdokids.com and access crafts, games, videos and more!

Abdo Kids Code:
HAK9251